Master Your Mental Sufferings

Collection of Essays by

Daksh Jindal

Copyrights

Master Your Mental Sufferings

First edition. July 29, 2024.

Written by Daksh Jindal.

Prologue

Over 10 years I have read 200+ books on philosophy, psychology and biographies. These books gave me the mental framework to fight all the mental sufferings from anxiety, overthinking, heart break, fear of death to porn addiction.

Through these essays, I want to take you inside the thinking process to deal with these modern mental sufferings and help you build a psychological framework with some real life actions to help you master your mental sufferings.

Don't read this book cover to cover. Just pick one essay and dive deep into it. Read it, contemplate on it and implement it in your life. Don't read to finish the book but to absorb the book as much as you can.

I am sure one of the essays will become your mental guide during difficult times, helping you master your mental sufferings and make you live a more peaceful life. Happy Reading !!!

Prologue
Anxiety About Future
She Rejected Me
Fear of Death
Choose Your Suffering
Ambition Steals Your Present
Fool The Fear
Looking For Love
Loving Discipline
Patience Is Our Natural State
Getting True Strength Back
Comparison The Killer of Happiness
The Power Of Intentions
How To Change Your Reality
Building A Rich Mindset
Anger Management
Thinking Big In Life
I Am Jealous Of Everyone
Porn Addiction
Who Are You?
Acknowledgements
Thank You

Anxiety About Future

Essay 1

I have been going through anxiety since last few weeks. This anxiety is due to multiple fears, ranging from fear of changing my career path to the fear of death.

Anxiety about the career arising from my decision to leave a very well paid job for pursuing a risky career in social media.

My greedy mind showing me how much money I will loose by doing this and making me anxious by putting all the negative scenarios in my imagination where I am begging for money to help my family survive and regretting the risk that I took in life.

Anxiety about death specially after seeing my dad pass away. Before that, death was just a distant thing that happened to others and could never happen to me. But after my dad, death felt very close to home. Something that can come for me anytime and separate me from all my loved ones in the blink of an eye.

I feel my heart racing as my mind goes down into an uncontrollable spiral of thoughts.

The pressure of productivity is also having an opposite effect on my mental health. It makes me feel that I am wasting my time if I do anything that does not align with my long term goals.

It feels like my life has become a treadmill, I need to keep running on, until I achieve my future goals. Honestly I will never achieve my future goals because I know my ambition will keep creating a new future with new goals. This keeps me in constant anxiety. This is something I needed to work on.

When all these anxieties take over my mind, they create a havoc in my body and makes me feel helpless. It makes the life feel meaningless and all the big dreams and ambitions feel distant. The future becomes unreachable due to all the pressure from career choices, death and productivity.

Anxiety makes your mind your biggest enemy. As it did to mine. But going through all this I realised one thing, the biggest reason for all my anxieties was my aim to live every moment for the future which I had no control over.

My days were completely optimised to work on things that will be good for me in the future. A future which I just agreed will keep changing with new goals.

What a stupid way to spend my everyday, chasing an illusion which I myself will keep changing, the closer I get to it. No wonder anxiety never leaves me.

All these thoughts gave me the eureka moment I needed. What if I started doing few things not for the illusory future but for the very real present day.

Things that brought the depth of happiness and satisfaction today rather than keeping me anxious about the results that I will get tomorrow.

What could be that thing? A small walk in the park near by, touching the trees, looking at the sky and listening to the kids laughing and playing.

Doing it, not with the intention of getting anything from it in the future. Doing it just with the intention of getting maximum happiness out of it today.

I tried and surprise, it reduced my anxiety and made me realise that I need to have more guilt free leisure time during the day where I don't care about what I am doing or where I am going as long as I am doing something ethical and joyful.

I will go on a random walk without worrying about the destination, I will play random music and dance to it, I will read a random book from my bookshelf with no intention of finishing it, I will draw a random piece of art, I will do what I feel like in that moment rather than worrying about the future goals or future success.

We need to increase the depth of our everyday experience. This means living less in the future and more in the now.

Guilt free leisure activity that we do to get happiness today rather than a false hope of happiness tomorrow will be the key to reduce anxiety and increase the quality of our everyday lives.

She Rejected Me

Essay 2

I met her on a trip to a beautiful English village. At first look she seemed like a typical English girl, red cheeks, beautiful eyes and very fit. I never knew this trip would get us so close intellectually.

The trip was for 4 days but those 4 days seemed like 4 lifetimes I spent with her. I never wanted that trip to end. We started with a long drive to the village where I sat with her at the back seat.

We talked about everything from British politics to her research work. The most attractive part of her was that she was curious to know my opinion about everything.

She was unlike any other girl who just wanted to be heard and only loved talking. She was different she liked asking questions just the way I did, she was curious about my opinion rather than just talking about herself and her own life. This was the first time this ever happened to me. In every relationship I have ever been I was the only curious one and the the girl just loved talking.

Her curiosity combined with her love for nature made her even more beautiful. She loved walking for hours and hours just like I did. During those walks while our friends were busy with their own talks, me and her bonded beautifully.

We talked about our families, our intellectual passions, our life goals. This was the first time I never flirted with a girl I was attracted to. I always wanted to wake up early in the morning and go to bed late, to spend as much time with her as possible.

I think she enjoyed my company as well. I could sense it from her talks, from her small gestures of trying to be with me at certain moments on the trip.

Everything was perfect as the trip was about to end, we promised each other to go out for coffee and the way she said "I would love that." It just melted my heart.

But the connection and the vibes we had on the trip didn't take long to disappear when we got back to our normal lives. We stayed in touch through texts as we talked about books. I asked her for coffee and she agreed but then something changed and she never came for the coffee. I felt rejected and heartbroken.

This rejection started making me see the whole British society as racist not letting other skin colour people into their lives. ***Rejection can be a silent poison sowing seeds of hatred in your heart*** and that is what started happening to me.

My British best friend who has been so supportive to me for 7 years, I started seeing him differently. That small phase of rejection would have taken me down a completely different road in life if I hadn't brought myself back to my senses by counting all the happy moments this country has given me.

All the love people of this country have shown me, from my university professors to my office colleagues and to my neighbours. They all accepted me like a family.

This reality check made me appreciate my life in Britain. It also made me realise that as love blinds, rejection can also blind you.

You can start painting everyone with the same colour of hatred, as the poison of rejection takes root inside you. Like a girl getting rejected by a man could start hating all the men and vice versa.

We need to be very careful with this feeling and give ourselves a reality check again and again by counting the blessings of the people who accepted us.

So do I hate that girl now? No. Yes she rejected me but neither she nor anyone else can take away the time we spent together in that English village. She taught me what intellectual and emotional attachment actually feels like and how it is more important than any physical attraction that we can have just for bodily pleasures.

I miss her curiosity but I am sure the way I wasn't prepared for her to enter my life, there would be many more people and experiences that I am not prepared for yet. I am looking forward to those.

Fear of Death

Essay 3

When my dad was on his death bed fighting COVID. He was in a crowded hospital where the doctors had given up on his treatment. My dad feeling breathless, asked the doctor "Doctor, everyone is getting cured. Why am I suffering?" He didn't want to die. He wanted to be cured.

He took his last breath in an ambulance, while being transported to another hospital, with his head on my brother's lap. I received a call with the news "He was no more." I couldn't believe it. I thought death is something that happened to others and it will never touch us anytime soon.

I was confused, devastated, sad, worried. All the emotions clouded my mind. I still couldn't believe this has happened and was expecting a call saying "Good news, somehow the doctors got him on the ventilator and he made it." Hours passed by and the reality sunk in. The reality that the conversation I

had with him yesterday was the last conversation we ever had.
This was my first close meeting with death. Then after few months when COVID passed away, a new form of death started taking over the news. Heart attacks specially amongst the people of my age.

How someone lost consciousness in the gym and was declared dead in few hours. How someone fainted during a dance performance and was declared dead. How someone walking into a college fell down due to a heart failure and died. Even writing about this right now gives me some kind of shiver.

And then the inevitable happened. On my second trip to India after cremating my dad in the first trip. I reached home expecting to help my family move on after 1 year. On my first night in Delhi, I fainted and got hospitalised. It was COVID. All the fears completely overtook me.

At that point one particular book that helped me was The Power of Positive Thinking which kept me alive in my mind during the difficult time.

After going through this, I started my journey to kill the fear of death completely. For that I started reading and listening to the interviews of people who faced death everyday, from battlefield warriors to the astronauts. What made them so strong to face death and still get big courageous things done?

I found my answer in this poem

"Do not go gentle into that good night,
Old age should burn and rave at close of day;
Rage, rage against the dying of the light....."

This was the mantra that the warriors/astronauts/civil right activists followed who were risking their lives everyday. This mantra simply means death (night) will come and get you one day or the other.

Will the death find you scared in your bed trying to get away from it? Or will it find you raging and changing your body, mind and the world? The choice is ours, will we go into the good night scared or raging?

This was the mindset all the warriors/astronauts/activists followed. When the death comes will they be in their bed scared and lazy or will they be in the world taking big actions to change it with their body and mind. How would they go into this good night? Raging or lazing around.

This simple poem shifted my mindset. Whenever I was at the gym and the fear of heart attack came to my mind, I asked my self "Will the death find me fighting with metal to work on my body, or will it find me scared in my bed watching Netflix."

The answer came "If it comes today it will find me fighting the metal and raging in the gym."

This has become my mantra whenever I feel I am doing something risky that could bring me closer to death. I ask myself "Will I go raging into the good night? Or lazing into the good night?" The answer is always raging.

Remember these 3 lines, memorise them and the fear of death will never touch you again.

"Do not go gentle into that good night,
Old age should burn and rave at close of day;
Rage, rage against the dying of the light....."

By Dylan Thomas

Choose Your Suffering

Essay 4

Standing in the heat of the sun, distributing pamphlets for my coding classes for kids, getting rejected by people again and again. I questioned myself "I have a job at one of the most prestigious companies in the world, I am earning a decent salary and I can afford most of the things that people can only think of. Then why am I suffering like this in the middle of the day?"

I ask this question to myself everytime I take a bold decision in my life. "Why are you making life so difficult for yourself? Why can't you just enjoy life the way everyone enjoys? Go on holidays, buy expensive things and show other people how successful you are. Why do you walk towards suffering all the time?"

My mind replies, suffering is the final destination of our every desire. When we desire for anything in life we attach suffering to it by default. I realised this with my desire to marry the girl I fell in love with. Everyday she fought with me, it made me suffer with the thought that she might leave me. Everyday she talked to another guy it made me suffer with the feeling of jealousy and insecurity.

I face suffering with my desire to become a social media entrepreneur, to make a change in the society. As noble as the cause sounds, it doesn't reduce the suffering I face with every failure in my journey. Suffering is an everyday companion I have learnt to live with.

Running requires me to suffer, by pushing my physical limits. Reading too much makes me suffer in my social life, as it has become difficult for me to keep up with the normal gossip that people call conversation. My mind is always looking for intellectual stimulation which normal people provide me very less with.

Does this mean there is no point in choosing the difficult path of discipline as it's full of suffering? No. If I didn't choose that path then I would follow the path that the world wants me to follow.

Watching Netflix, scrolling mindlessly, buying more things to show how successful I am. If I live through this undisciplined life, it gives me an illusion that it's filled with the happiness. Instead I will just be finding an escape with temporary pleasure. I will loose touch with the real life.

Real life is using my mind to solve problems, using my body to play and become stronger. Using my eyes to admire nature and sunsets, using my lips to speak the right words with our loved ones and help them in their goals.

But all this comes at a cost of being vulnerable, ability to handle the suffering by making my mind vulnerable to study hard things, making my body vulnerable by fighting with metal, making my soul vulnerable by interacting with other people.

Vulnerability will lead to suffering. Some books will hurt my mind as they will be too difficult, exercise might injure me as I try to become stronger, people might betray me as I try to help them.

So most people choose to run away from these sufferings by escaping their real life through instant pleasures. Instant pleasures which will make me mentally dumb, physically fat, conversations filled with gossip, life filled with unnecessary mental problems due to my focus on what other people say and do. These illusions of pleasures actually leave us hollow from inside. We loose respect for ourself. Society looses respect for us. Our children won't call us their heroes.

Whereas when I choose to walk towards the suffering of my choice instead of what the world wants me to choose. Then that suffering brings meaning to my life.

Choosing my own suffering instead of the illusions of short term pleasures created by the world has made me mentally resilient and socially attractive with my knowledge and my will to take action.

So standing in the heat of the Sun, getting rejected by people while distributing pamphlets for my coding classes, I remind myself

"This is the suffering of building something beautiful that I am choosing to walk towards, rather than the hollowness of short term pleasures, the world wants me to choose."

Ambition Steals Your Present

Essay 5

Ambition is a boon and a curse in itself. Everyone knows the boon part and that is all the books and media amplify. But very few people talk about the curse it brings with itself.

I have noticed that living ambitiously has slowly stole my present away from me. Every activity which I do with an ambitious mind, I do it *not* for the enjoyment of that activity but for the bright future that activity will bring in my life.

This is a very anxious and result dependent way of living. This way you are always in an expectation mode. This expectation mode keeps you anxious about the results which could go either ways.

You forget to enjoy the activity that you are doing. *Your whole purpose to live in the present moment gets diverted to achieving a brighter future.* Which is completely wrong, the purpose for anything I do in the present moment should be to live that present moment completely.

This is what I feel "Going with the flow" means. To be in the flow state to enjoy that moment rather than expecting to get something out of that moment. When you attach expectations to that moment *you malign the flow state* and it just becomes a means to an end rather than an end in itself.

So the best way to live your life ambitiously is by forgetting your ambition in your everyday moments and doing things in those moments for the pleasure of doing them rather than with the expectation of getting something out of it in the future.

If you are reading history, read it to enjoy that moment, if you are shooting a video, shoot it to enjoy that moment without expecting anything else from it.

So what I learnt is that use your ambition to set long term goals but to achieve those long term goals, *build enjoyable habits and then forget about your long term goal.*

Enjoying those habits should become your primary goal so that you can be in the moment without any expectations, without any anxiety about the future and experience it completely because that moment is your end goal. *Your ambitious future is just a byproduct of you enjoying those moments.*

Fool The Fear

Essay 6

Fear is your everyday companion, always in a conversation with you whenever you are alone. It waits for you to think big or do something uncomfortable so that it can dominate you and stop you from taking even the first step.

Fear can become a tyrant enemy that can whip you to it's own wishes and make you conform to your most mediocre self. If you don't stand up for yourself, fear will take away everything from you, from your health and wealth to your most sacred thing your *self respect*.

Fear has been the biggest reason behind my procrastination. Whenever I think of doing anything new in life, my fear kicks in. It makes me feel "You will never be able to create your own education system." "Don't make that video, it will never work." "Don't write this book no one will ever read it."

As soon as I start listening to it, that's it I am done. It points me to an easier option of distraction and eats up all my time. This is the loop I struggle with every-time I think of doing anything new. Breaking this loop is the key to push myself to take actions in new direction and create depth in various field.

That is why the most important thing I am learning, is to show fear it's true place. ***Fear should be no more than a wise advisor to me. Advising me about the worst case scenario and helping me plan for it.***

Once my planning is done and I prepare for the worst case scenario, if the fear still tries to dominate me by reminding me the worst case again and again, I am learning to stand up to it. By fooling the fear.

To fool the fear, right words are the key. Words create real magic. What is the secret behind "Gandhi ji" "Ambedkar ji" "Modi ji's" influence on such a mass scale? Words.

Words create emotions and emotions make us act in a certain way. Right words from these leaders made people act in the most unexpected ways that we couldn't even imagine doing few years back.

So when fear starts putting in negative words in my mind, it starts creating the feelings of failure, looser, not good enough etc and these feelings have pushed me many times to find an escape in distractions like social media.

To get out of this paralysing effect I have started fooling fear with the right words. When I want to make a video and fear says no one will watch it, I reply "It's okay. I just want 1 person to watch it." Fear feels that is easy and can happen easily, Okay I will let you do it.

Similarly when I want to study for an exam, fear says "You will never clear this exam, stop studying." I reply "Okay. I will study just 1 paragraph and try to understand what it is trying to say." Fear again feels that is easy, Okay I will let you do it.

That's it as soon as I take that small step, momentum and flow state transports me to a world of just beautiful action and learning, everything starts feeling easy and the universe smiles at me for taking action once again.

A fearful man caves into his emotional self, over analysing, paralysed to take action and looking for pleasurable escapes instead of fighting fear head on. I have been in this situation many times where I lost my precious consciousness into garbage scrolling just to escape fears.

But after learning from the giants like Gandhi, Churchill, Elon and Lincoln, I am training myself to fool fear everyday. Use it as a wise advisor to prepare for the worst case and after that, fool it by suggesting it the small doable action.

As soon as you take that small step the fear disappears, momentum kicks in helping you convert that small action into a big brave step towards your ambitious goal.

Looking For Love

Essay 7

I have been feeling a little lonely these last few days as there is no one to talk to at home. Someone I can share my thoughts with and may be feel home with. Sometimes it feels like an anchor is missing in my life. Someone I can return to everyday and see them smile and talk with me.

I don't know if this is a romanticised dream that has got planted in my mind due to the media feeding us a picture of happy life where you have a partner and you live happily ever after.

I can't even imagine how my mom feels after my dad passed away. I miss him too as he was a big part of my life. Someone I can call at the middle of the night and feel safe with but honestly he was not a part of my everyday routine. But for my mom he was everything. It is surprising how committing to a single person all your life can make them such a big part of your life. You share so many memories and moments that you forever cherish.

But on the other hand does having a partner really improves your everyday life experience? Or does it just provide you with a *psychological safety* that you have someone with you.

I feel okay when my housemate (someone I am sharing my house with) is around, it gives me that psychological safety. So do we just spend life with each other only for that psychological safety? Is this what finding love really is?

Finding that psychological safe zone, where you can be yourself and it helps you grow at every level in life. Yes physical intimacy is also a big part of love but honestly on the timescale of spending 40 years of your life with someone, if you calculate the physical intimacy part it will hardly account for 20% (this too for guys with high sexual stamina. Lol). So majority of the relationship is about psychological safety.

If that is the case then can we build this psychological safety with ourselves? For that first we will have to define psychological safety. From my observation psychological safety is simply talking to someone about your deepest thoughts knowing that these things will remain between both of you and the other person will be a good listener. This process can be replicated with a diary and a pen where you can write every thought of yours and paper is a good listener.

Next aspect of psychological safety is to get good advise in return for us sharing our vulnerability. Can reading biographies and essays do the same? As they are effectively people talking to us and sharing their lifetime of experience.

What else comprises of psychological safety that requires us to have a human with us for lifetime? May be the fear of not being well and knowing there is someone to take care of us. Can that be replaced by a phone call to a friend?

Some unmeasurable aspects of psychological safety are the small things that the other person does for us from cooking something we like, to cheering us up by taking us outside. These small things are immeasurable may be.

But shouldn't we be doing those things for ourselves firstly? We should be loving ourselves and doing those small things for our self, out of self love and not expecting someone else to do it for us.

These expectations that we put on someone else, actually are the root cause of our own misery. Like my expectation from you to like this book. Is that why I am writing this book? If I do that I will only write the things that you want to hear like "Don't give up" "Universe has your back" etc. Because I will have neediness for you to like me.

This neediness takes away my originality and honesty. Shouldn't I be writing this book for myself as a guide during difficult time? That way I won't need your assurance and I will write what I honestly feel about life.

Same thing happens when we tell ourselves that we are lonely and we need someone. We make someone else responsible for our psychological safety and then comes the whole burden of expectations which never gets satisfied.

So if we conclude all the aspects of psychological safety: sharing thoughts, getting advice, fear of illness and small things out of love, these can all be fullfilled without having a person with you 24/7 in your life. Because people who lose their loved ones due to death actually practice all this to continue living a good life.

Hence our youth should not be wasted in finding love for the sake of psychological safety, instead it should be used to build that psychological safety independently and share it with the right person at the right time.

It is a difficult task to over come social conditioning of "finding the special one", but many greats have overcome it from Sir Isaac Newton to Leonardo Da Vinci and many future greats will, because it is the task worth pursuing.

Loving Discipline

Essay 8

Love is a very strong feeling and a good motivator. I remember going to the gym regularly because of a girl I had a crush on during my teenage. I remember going to the tuitions regularly because of my love for Maths.

Love can make us do unbelievable things, helping us bring out a different side of ours that we never thought that we had. This reminds me of a story of an Indian guy who cycled to Europe because of a girl he fell in love with.

Why am I talking about love so much? What does discipline has to do with it? Before thinking about those questions, let's ask ourselves? Why do we find discipline so difficult to follow? Why can't we just remain disciplined all our lives?

This is where love comes in. When we love someone we want to spend more time with that person. Similarly when we love doing something, we want to do that thing again and again. So we can develop a similar feeling of love for discipline? Imagine a life where you are completely in love with a disciplined day. All the things on your to do list gets done. You are able to achieve every fitness, education and financial goal. Is it even possible?

I did an experiment to check whether I can actually develop the feelings of love for discipline in a similar way we develop feelings for a person or a hobby. This was the result.

I aimed to be completely disciplined just 1 day of the week. On that particular day I worked on every goal I had on my to do list and at the end of the day I felt so accomplished and happy. Then rest of the week I was just lazy and wasting my time. But what I noticed during those lazy days that I started missing that 1 day of discipline (like the way we miss a person).

I started missing that day because that day made me feel happy and accomplished compared to the other lazy days which just left me with guilt. So I wanted that feeling of accomplishment again.

Hence I started being disciplined 2 days week, not out of compulsion but because of my feeling of missing those days and that feeling of accomplishment. Then rest 5 days when I was lazy, I started missing discipline even more as I started to fall in love with those those days where I was just studying, writing achieving my goals and feeling happy at the end.

This feeling of love for those disciplined days increased with time and suddenly the number of disciplined days started increasing as well, going upto 4 disciplined days every week. That is more that 50% of the whole year. I got so much done in those days by not forcing myself but by actually making myself love those discipline days with this small experiment.

Even today when I feel I don't feel like being disciplined, I go back to the same root of developing love for discipline again. This is similar to having someone who loves you in your life always and then suddenly you start taking them for granted.

Same thing happens to discipline, I start taking those disciplined days for granted as I forget their importance and the way they make me feel. So I give myself space from my love. Just the way a couple needs space sometimes to re ignite that spark of love and romance.

I become undisciplined completely for 6 days and bring back discipline to just 1 day a week. The same psychological loop repeats, where the guilt of laziness from 6 days makes me hate those days whereas the happy feeling of a single disciplined day, attracts me towards it. I want to spend time with it more, I want to be happy more often.

Hence I fall in love with discipline again. This psychological hack has helped me see discipline, as my life partner I need to be close to and sometimes need to maintain distance from to get close again.

So now instead of cursing myself, forcing myself to become disciplined every day of my life and ending up hating my partner. I fell in love with discipline every week by aiming to spend time with it 4 days a week and missing it the next 3 days craving to get back to it again.

When you develop the feeling of love for something, you don't have to force yourself to spend time with them. Make discipline the first love of your life by seeing it as someone who will

give you happiness if you don't force yourself into it.

Patience Is Our Natural State

Essay 9

What is patience? Does patience means waiting and letting the universe give you what you deserve? Is it about waiting for the right time to take action? Or is it about waiting for the results from your hardwork?

Patience has been the most difficult skill to develop and yet it has been the most natural skill I had whenever I did things right. Patience freed me from anxiety about the results or future success and helped me live a more meaningful life.

How can patience be the most difficult and the most natural skill at the same time? Well patience becomes difficult when we commit to long term goals and face multiple failures and rejections on the way.

I remember applying to get my first job and the amount of rejections I went through. I was receiving atleast one rejection everyday in my mailbox.

All the hardwork and extra efforts I had put in at my university during evenings felt like a waste. When all my rich friends were having a good time in their evenings, I was studying or working on an engineering project.

When all my rich friends were going home during Christmas holidays, I was alone in the university hostel studying. But all of this was looking like a waste as despite all the hardwork only thing I was getting was rejection.

Being patient at such a time felt very difficult. Even my teenage was flashing back in front of my eyes. When I was 15, studying while sitting at my dad's grocery shop serving customers with cigarettes, while they smoke right in front of my face. I tried ignoring the smoke in front of my face and brought my focus back on the next mathematical problem I was trying to solve.

Then suddenly I had to go and deliver a bottle of 20 litres of water, carrying it on my shoulder to 3rd floor of a building, coming back and trying to focus on my studies again. All of this childhood hardwork seemed like a waste in front of those job rejections.

When you are going through a difficult time without getting results despite all the extra ordinary efforts that you have put in, impatience and anxiety become second nature.

Then why did I say that it is the most natural thing at the same time? How can it be natural when it is so difficult? Let me explain.

When do we require patience? When we are doing the most unnatural thing that a human is made to do, that is wait. Humans are not wired to wait else we would feel healthy both physically and mentally while waiting. But do we? No.

We feel physically and mentally healthy only when we are busy using our body and our mind. When we use our body for any purpose, from getting groceries to going for a walk we feel good. When we use our mind to plan a birthday party for someone or to solve a problem in our studies, we feel good. Hence movement is the most natural state of a human being.

Then where does patience fit in? How is this all related to patience? Think about it, if human beings stay in their natural state all the time then they can be patient easily as the don't waste their time waiting for the results but they are busy moving their body and their mind.

When we do that, we don't care about the results and the results happen automatically in the background. Patience becomes the natural state of taking action rather than waiting and getting frustrated.

Confused? Well let's get back to when I was getting rejected for jobs. If I would have fallen back to the waiting state which most people call patience, I would have applied to 10 may be 20 jobs and then just waited to get selected. If would have gotten rejected, I would have said this is my fate and stopped searching for jobs completely.

But since for me patience was the act to keep myself moving, I did just that. I kept applying for more and more jobs and bingo. I got the job and my life completely changed after that.

So patience is the most natural state of a human being. Where one does not wait for results to

happen and one does not stop taking action, improving on those actions and results happen as a byproduct, changing our lives completely.

Getting True Strength Back

Essay 10

Being born as human comes at a price of consistent hard work and keeping the mind in check. It is a privilege that our ancestors made full use of.

Like the Vikings for whom the doors of heaven would only open if they died in the battle field or the Spartans for whom any weakness in men was a matter of shame. They trained their kids from childhood to eradicate fear and laziness from their mind.

Similarly in all the ancient civilisations kids, teenagers and young adults were not raised in the comforts of supermarkets, cars and phones. They woke up every day at the break of dawn to help their parents in their vocations from cutting wood to hunting.

In our modern civilisation we are losing this strong character of hard work and discipline and instead drowning ourselves in the pleasures of comforts.

The comforts of our beds, the comfort of our phone and the comfort of unhealthy delicacies which are just a click away. This lifestyle is making us loose our true strength and making us soft and week.

In Vikings mythology one could only go to Valhalla (heaven) if one died fighting in the battlefield. Similarly Bhagwad Gita says one only gets closer to the Supreme Power when one dedicates his life to his work without any expectations of the results (Karma Yoga).

If our ancestors were still alive they would be disheartened at our laziness and how easily we have surrendered our body and minds to the unhealthy comforts of life. They would respect the birds more, who still wake up in time everyday and work for their food and survival all day.

The birds are in the battlefield everyday getting closer to Valhalla and Krishna. Whereas you and I are lost giving pleasure to our minds through our mindless consumption of media all day.

So I am taking back control by investing in a basic phone and it has given me significant results already. This phone only has whatsapp and spotify. The main phone with all the social media stays hidden in the house. It only comes out twice during the day for business purposes. Getting back my control over my focus and attention is the first step towards getting back on the battlefield.

The second step to get closer to the warrior mindset is by creating lack of money. Now all my money is either invested or donated. This keeps me in a frugal mindset of cooking my own food and buying only the necessities every week. The comfort of phone and money has been cut down from my life.

The last comfort is the comfort of bed which I have targeted by changing the timezone in my basic phone which keeps me 1 hour ahead of rest of the country I live in. Hence no snoozing can now stop me from waking up early and going to bed in time.

The comfort of phone, money and bed were making me weak but my desire to reach Valhalla or closer to Krishna is much more than a mediocre comfortable life. Hence I will keep fighting like a true warrior everyday for the things I believe in against the enemies like laziness, fear, mindless consumption and human corruption through my healthy habits and honest words. The question is will you?

Comparison The Killer of Happiness

Essay 11

At the age of 28 I have realised that happiness relies on the bare minimum things that nature has already provided us with. Why are the Buddhist monk the happiest people in the world? Why are people in the villages much happier than the people in the cities.

It is because happiness actually needs only 4 things that they all have: sense of community, nature, good health and meaningful work. A Buddhist monk is busy reading, meditating and taking care of the nature around him. This gives him intellectual stimulation as well as a sense of service in preserving something that is giving him life. Similarly people in the villages are busy growing food which gives them a strong sense of duty and plenty of time to spend with nature.

Whereas the people in the cities are busy finding happiness in the artificial things that we keep buying for comparison and these artificial things give us meaningless jobs in meaningless companies which are destroying our planet and our environment.

We know all this but we still fall in this infinite loop of buying more things because of the constant comparison that media teaches us to do.

This comparison actually pushes us away from the bare minimum things that we need to be happy. Those jobs pull us away from our homes and our communities, those material things pull us away from the shade of a tree or a bath in the river.

This constant race of comparison keeps us unsatisfied with what we have achieved till now and keeps us hungry for more and more and more till we get on our death bed and we realise that we spent our whole lives running behind the wrong things.

We realise that we always had the things we needed to be happy but we ran away from them in the search of a mythical ever happy state by owning as many things as we can, isolating ourselves from the loved ones and killing the planet in return.

So how can we get out of this race? Does this mean that we all should leave our jobs and move back to villages? Well the bus has already left the stop so there is no going back. But this does not mean we still can't do anything right now.

Simple solution to this is that don't pursue money to buy more things, pursue money to help more people and help the environment. This simple change of direction will add so much meaning to your life pulling you out of the race of comparison and taking you to the core root of happiness.

Using your money and skills to help the orphanages near your house buy spending 5% of your monthly time and income with them, or spending time with the old age homes or spending time with the farmers on a weekend and helping them on their farms or may be spending that time and money with the animal shelters.

This simple shift in attitude will help you get closer to the real community, will bring you closer to nature, will add meaning to your work and keep you mentally and physically active.

This type of weekend is much better than shallow drunk nights that only lead you to hangovers and wrong decisions that we regret all our lives.

Don't you feel hollow even after buying that phone you always wanted to buy because others had it? Don't you feel hollow thinking that no matter how much I get in life there will always be someone richer than me? Don't you feel hollow doing a job that you have no interest in just for the money it provides?

It's a sign that you need to get back to the 4 main core pillars of happiness community, nature, health and meaningful work. I made the jump I hope you do too.

The Power Of Intentions

Essay 12

I feel intentions are the key to unlocking the mysteries of the universe. Intentions connects you to the super intelligence which guides you and opens doors for you.

The right intentions will take you to the peak of any career whereas wrong intentions will keep you swimming in the muddy waters of mediocrity.

What are right and wrong intentions? Thinking only about your own gains and pleasures lead you to the road of wrong intentions. When you do a work with an expectation to get something out of it instead of the love you have for the work, you are working with wrong intentions.

Thinking about the gain of the whole company/ society/family will lead you to the road of right intentions. When you do the work without any expectations and just for the love of doing that work, you are working with right intentions.

Simple example to prove this. When a high school student joins the university to become an engineer he has so many dreams about changing the world like Elon Musk and Jeff Bezoz.

But then he drowns into the university environment where everyone is studying with the intention of getting a job and a good salary rather than studying with a fascination for learning.

This change in intentions leads to a competitive mindset where student now studies day and night under this pressure loosing all his enthusiasm that he had at the start. This change in intention drains him of his energy and he just wants to finish education and never look back at it again.

Now the same student joins a job where his intention gets completely moulded again. At workplace everyone is talking about promotions, salary increments and holidays.

Everyone is focused on the intention on how can they get maximum money out from the company for their own pleasures. The intention of giving the company their best work to help it grow fades away. This leads to a company run by undedicated employees trying to find shortcuts just to make more money.

These employees in their personal life now use this money to keep up with the comparison culture they learnt from the university and the company.

They buy things they don't need like cars, shoes, fancy clothes and they cut themselves off from the things they actually need like the community, nature, family etc. The intention here is to maximise material wealth to buy more things and use those things as a badge of honour.

Whereas everyone forgets that history only remembers the people whose work was their badge of honor. History doesn't remember the king with the biggest castle, but the king who made the most difficult decisions and did the most honest work in his life time from Lord Ram to Marcus Aurelius.

If the intention was changed slightly from "I need to make more money to buy more things." to "I need to make more money to help more people."

everything will change in that employees life from his habits to his lifestyle.

He will start reading books, watching videos around how can he help more people using his current privileged situation. He will start going to the NGOs and helping out on the weekends rather than using that time and money to party and poison his body with alcohol.

I was one of these employees. But once I changed my intentions, I saw the magic of the universe.

How the universe made me succeed in anything that I started with the intention of giving back to the society, from my free classes to teach kids how to code to starting my own education system online in order to help people become mentally and emotionally strong.

The universe has stepped in and unlocked doors for me on every platform I visited. Whereas if I would have started social media or any business with the intention of becoming rich and famous I am sure I would still be struggling and probably would have given up.

Even till today I tell the Universe, the day my intention becomes selfish, take everything away from me as I won't deserve any of it. So intentions are my true guiding force in life and I hope after reading this you also set your intentions right.

How To Change Your Reality

Essay 13

Before changing the reality we need to understand what is reality? Are we all living in the same reality? Can we actually change reality?

Let's start with the first question, what is reality?

Our reality is not the world that we see, hear or touch. Our reality is the world that we create in our mind by attaching stories and judgements to the things that we see, hear and touch.

Is the reality same for everyone?

Well from the outside it seems like we all are living in the same reality. You are reading the same letters that I am writing. But from the inside we all are living in our own unique realities.

Some of you reading this might find my words as gold, guiding you in some way. But some of you might find these words absolute garbage. So your reality is not these words written on this paper, but it is how you interpret these words in your mind and give meaning to them.

It is similar to you enjoying your favourite street food whereas another person hating the same food due to getting sick by it previously. Here the food is same but it is the story about the food that is different in everyone's mind.

Can we change the reality?

So if we focus on changing the reality outside, we will never be successful as the reality outside is same for everyone. Every one will go through the pain of losing their parents, the fear of failing in exams, the negative thinking due to past failures. This reality due to external events is same for everyone. But it is how you interpret these harsh realities of life that decides the action you take in your life which decides the new reality you create for yourself.

So changing the reality simply means changing the mental interpretation of negative and painful events in your life. I developed this skill by reading stories about people who have gone through even worse situations in their lives, like Dr Victor Frankl in A Man's Search For Meaning where he lost each and every member of his family due to Hitler and the Nazis but how he channeled that pain to keep himself alive and make the best of his life.

Similarly a story about a black slave girl from The Underground Railroad, where she leaves her kids behind in a farm to escape slavery and how the pain of separation and the brutal treatment of her slave friends gave her the courage to fight the system and build a new life.

Reading such painful stories makes you grateful about your own life and helps you interpret your painful experiences in a better way. Like when I lost my dad Victor Frankl's story gave me courage helping me look at the brighter side making me realise that I am fortunate enough to still have most of my family alive.

So instead of crying all the time and feeling victimised I accepted the reality with a strong heart that my dad had to leave me one day or the other.

Now it is my duty to make the most of this life he has gifted me and make him proud.

This simple change in interpretation in my mind helped me change my reality where a difficult incident in my life became my strength instead of my weakness and this in turn helped me take better decisions like moving back to India and taking the riskier path of building a new education system because I know I will also die and I need to make the best of this life my dad has gifted me. Instead of staying safe in a job and just enjoying my life by travelling and buying more things.

So changing the interpretation of the most painful moments of your life, helps you change your reality. To practice this skill read as many stories of inspiring people who have had a painful life instead of watching music and movies where they show money, alcohol, drugs and smoking are the only way to escape the pain.

Building A Rich Mindset

Essay 14

Growing up in a middle class household, seeing your uncles and cousins getting richer and richer whereas your own family is still stuck where it was 10 years back was really painful. This perspective towards life made me develop negative emotions towards my dad whom I though was not working hard enough. He was just happy with what we had.

Whereas my cousins were buying a Mercedes Benz. At that time I started dreaming of becoming rich one day and owning everything that my cousins have.

This was the beginning of my poor mindset. With time I started seeing my rich friends and cousins with envy and jealousy and these negative feelings started filling me up more with the ambition of getting rich. The only thing I wanted in my life was never to become like my dad who never achieved anything in his life.

This poor mindset pushed me towards pursuing my education more seriously. I went abroad and studied robotics engineering risking all my dad's saving to pursue my dream of becoming rich as an engineer.

Fortunately I was good at maths and this helped me go through my university life with the arrogance that no one can stop me from becoming rich now.

I finished my degree and got a really well paid job. Money started flowing in. I bought a house at the age of 23 and that was another boost to my ego that I am rich.

But then settling into the job I started talking to all the employees who have been working in the company for 20-30 years and they told me how they hated their jobs and the only reason they were there was to get a salary.

The only thing everyone talked about was going for the next big holiday or buying the next fancy car. I started sensing something was wrong, life can't be only about getting into this loop of getting a bigger car and a bigger house.

I am sure Einstein, Steve Jobs, Elon Musk didn't live their lives like this. What did they do differently. After reading their biographies I realised a common pattern amongst the people who actually did something significant in their lives. They were satisfied with what they had. They never craved for material things, they only craved for hard work in order to improve the lives of people around them.

Then the reality hit me. My dad whom I started to dislike for *not* wanting more in life actually had the richest mindset in all the family. He was happy with all the material things he had but he wanted to work hard to improve the lives of his kids.

Because of his frugal living I got the opportunity to go abroad whereas now most of my cousins are struggling with alcohol addictions and abundance of money but lack of purpose and lack of hard work in life.

My dad's frugal lifestyle taught me that finding contentment in the things you already have and finding ambition in helping the people around you through your hard work is the real rich mindset.

The answer to the rich mindset was always in front of me but the glorification of greed in today's culture had made me blind towards it.

This made me realise an engineer should become an engineer not to get a job and good salary to buy more things, no but to make this world a better place by helping his company walk towards sustainable engineering.

Similarly an accountant should not aim to make more money by teaching people how to evade tax, instead he should focus on inspiring people on how to pay the tax honestly to help the country develop.

Similarly every profession can be changed from satisfying your greed to helping the society. So focusing on becoming rich by changing the lives of people with your hard work instead of getting into the never ending loop of buying things is the true foundation of a rich mindset.

Anger Management

Essay 15

I don't get angry too often but today was the day when the hot tempered teenager in me came out after a long time. This hot tempered teenager is alive in all of us.

He comes out speaking vengeful words, making wrong decisions and taking irresponsible actions that we regret all our life. This teenager in me came out today and he wanted to take control and set everything right in the most verbally violent way.

If I would have let the teenager take over me, I would have regretted my whole life repeating the mistakes of my past again and again. It would have ruined my relationship that I hold very dear and it would have made me lose faith and trust in the opposite gender. But all the reading, all the teaching and all the practice of years helped me today.

When that teenager takes over, we can't argue with him. They always think that they are right. Same thing was happening to my mind and my thoughts. That teenager inside me was poisoning my mind with vengeful thoughts and was trying to push me to take irresponsible actions that I definitely would have regretted later.

So there was no point arguing with that teenager in my mind because he was very stubborn and arrogant and only looking for revenge like every other teenager. So I reminded myself that if that teenager owns my mind, I own my body. Let him speak and fill me up with negative energy, I won't let that negative energy come out of me through wrong actions.

So I decided to run. I decided to run till my legs get tired and that teenager stopped talking to me. Also while running I knew I couldn't talk to that teenager as he won't listen to me but I knew he would listen to the people he respected. Naval Ravikanth was one of those.

So I put on a podcast with Naval's interview and I ran and I ran till my legs started hurting and surprisingly by the time that happened, Naval had convinced the angry teenager that what he was trying to do was incorrect.

Naval told him how this life is so short and the only good way to use the time is by keeping yourself busy in the loop of learning and implementing. Naval put his life in perspective and reminded him how no one will remember him if he kept using this negative energy for wrong actions and if he kept getting distracted from his goals like this.

The teenager in me calmed down and my body and mind felt so much lighter after that good run. That run and Naval's podcast saved me from making angry decisions and taking wrong actions with the intention of revenge.

So make sure you learn to handle the teenager inside you similarly. Take his aggression out through a productive physical activity, tiring your body and help him see the bigger picture by making him listen to the people he respects. ***Anger is just the teenager shouting inside you, don't give into his demands. Instead help him mature.***

Thinking Big In Life

Essay 16

Does thinking big makes you greedy? Does thinking big overwhelms you and makes you anxious? Well thinking big has always been a integral part of my life. And yes it did make me greedy and anxious specially when I had an immature understanding of thinking big in life.

The society taught me that thinking big was imagining yourself flooded with money and everyone knowing your name. The way the news and media describes Elon Musk is worth Rs 4000cr. These stories shaped my consciousness during my teenage.

So I started thinking big since I was a child, my first big dream was to become an Indian cricketer and people shouting my name as I walk into the ground.

That dream got shattered when I couldn't balance cricket with studies. My second big dream like any Delhiite was to become an actor. To act and mesmerise people and people shouting my name where ever I go. These big dreams were not really dreams but illusions based on 0 awareness of the ground reality. In the end I was disappointed both the times.

Similarly when I joined my company my next big dream was to become the CEO of the company. Sitting in a suit amongst the directors and executives making million dollar deals and coming to work in a Rolls-Royce car.

Again the immaturity of this dream only led me to disappointment. These big dreams were immature because of my lack of self education. Once I started reading, definition of thinking big in life completely changed for me.

I started recognising patterns in the lives of people who actually thought big and achieved big in their lives. I found these people in biographies. These people taught me that thinking big doesn't mean thinking about glory all the time. Thinking big actually meant giving selfless love to one particular field of profession in your life. This selfless love led to big things in life. Let me explain how.

Barack Obama didn't think big about becoming the President of USA he just selflessly loved working for the betterment of the American community. At one point in life, he slept in parks to do that.

This selfless love for the betterment of Americans made him realise he needs to study more to contribute, hence he ended up doing law and became an even more powerful activist because of it. This selfless love to the cause of the betterment of American life not the illusory thinking made him the President.

Similarly Steve Jobs selflessly loved the art of creating most beautiful and powerful computers on the planet. This selfless love to this cause made him take big ambitious steps in revolutionising the computing, mobile phone and music industries. He just selflessly loved making beautiful computers.

Same goes with the story of all the very good CEOs. They never just dreamt themselves to be the CEO but they selflessly loved their company so much that they wanted to work on improving company processes, helping other people grow.

They weren't in the complaining mode like all average employees complaining about manager, salary, work times etc. They were always in the problem solving mode. Every complaint that they heard in the company was an opportunity for them to improve the company.

So learning this completely changed the direction of my life. I started noticing my selfless love for Maths that made me a good engineer. Similarly my selfless love for reading and teaching that helped me start my social media.

So now I know the only way to think big in life is by expressing selfless love to a particular field. Your self less love is the best way to think big in life.

I Am Jealous Of Everyone

Essay 17

These days as I am getting closer to resigning from my job and moving back to India, my mind is going into scarcity mode. I am becoming jealous of everyone who has become successful already at a young age or to a similar age of mine.

My mind is trying to find ways to hate them by finding reasons to demean their hard work and labelling their work as "shallow" and labelling them as "lucky".

My mind is doing all this to make me feel better about my self. But what this is really doing is, creating unnecessary hatred inside me for that person just because they became successful before me.

I never thought of all this when I was secure in my job and was earning enough money knowing that I am safe and I have enough. But this uncertainty of leaving the job, is pulling me out of abundance mindset where I fear people who have already become financially comfortable are my enemies and my mind wants them to fall down. So that I can become successful before them and show the world how great I am.

If I look deeper into these thoughts, this scarcity mindset is there because of our 1000 years old mental wiring, as in the jungles if someone had more food than you, it meant he had better chances of mating and surviving.

In the modern time, this scarcity mindset is useless as the social situations have completely changed. There is abundance in every field of work from starting your own youtube channel to starting your own tea selling business.

You will always find customers if you have a good product. So instead of feeling jealous of my friends I should stand by their side and congratulate them for all their hard work.

I know it's easier said than done. Jealousy is that poison that only effects you, not the other person.

Once you drink that poison, it is very difficult to get it out of your system.

I will get this poison out, by reminding myself the teaching of Buddha "The duality of our mind creates desire and hatred." This means I am not jealous of my friends because they are successful, I am jealous of them because I desire to be successful too.

My feeling of desire to be successful is creating the feeling of jealousy (hatred). So this desire has cropped up during a vulnerable time in my life where I feel scared of leaving my job and losing financial stability in my life.

So it is this fear of lack of financial stability that is creating the desire of financial success which in turn creating the feeling of jealousy in my life. This fear is illusory because as long as I have a healthy mind and body, I can always use them to labor in any field and provide value to the society to get that financial stability.

My willingness to do labor even during the most fearful time of my life is the cure to my jealousy. Labor will cure the desire for financial success and will pull out all the poison of jealousy from my body. Labor is all we have and all we can give to this world. ***The world won't remember us for our jealousies but for the work we leave behind due to our willingness to labor our body and mind.***

Porn Addiction

Essay 18

I am one of the most sexually corrupt person. I have cheated on my past girlfriends many times, I have broken hearts of many girls who fell in love with me. This is the one side of me which I am least proud of. This is why I can never speak confidently about relationships when some asks me about them.

But let's investigate this weakness even more. Now you can quit this book thinking why am I even listening to this corrupt guy or we can both go on a journey of investigation to find the root for lust and how to manage it in our own lives.

During the initial days of living abraod whenever I went back home, my friends never asked me about how my studies were going or how was I adjusting in a new environment.

Instead their question was always "Did you loose your virginity? Did you have sex?" My answer for first few years was always an upsetting No. My success abroad was being measured by the amount of sex I had. My immature mind in my late teenage and early 20's accepted this as the reality of life. More sex is equal to more social acceptance in life.

So is the social pressure and my friend circle, the only two factors responsible for my missteps? No. Even during the school days we hardly learnt anything about the most essential human needs like building social connections, finding emotional fulfilment, developing discipline to achieve all our dreams and goals.

Similarly we learnt almost nothing about human psychology, how the mind works and how the companies and the modern culture tries to hook us into pleasurable escapes that you can't fight, as you lack the psychological tools to fight them.

I have suffered due to lack of education around these most essential human needs. Staying by myself for 10 years in an expensive country where most of my friends belonged to rich upper class and had the money to go out and socialise, the only place where I found people was on my laptop screen. It was the cheapest means for me to socialise at the beginning of my journey in an new expensive country driven by consumerism instead of simplicity.

You had to have money to socialise, as the only thing most people know and do is to keep themselves entertained by consuming, by going to expensive restaurants, expensive malls, talking about new gadgets they are going to buy etc etc. This whole mindset of consumerism isolated me to my screen as I had no confidence to face people or the money to go out and spend with them to become friends.

This started my journey of binge watching tv series through third party websites. Now came the exploitation of psychological loopholes by the media industry.

Being high on sexual hormones in my early 20's and lack of access to actual social groups and girl friends to date and learn from, I started indulging in popular adult tv series like Game of Thrones. Even the most decent comedy tv shows like Big Bang Theory had a pinch of sexuality added to it.

As the whole media industry knows that the best way to hook someone to anything is by adding "sex" to it. I am sure the title of this essay got your attention more than anything because of the word "porn" which just points to sex.

Am I going into a complaining attitude by blaming everyone except myself? Yes I am.

I am blaming everyone for that stage of my life, my social group where maximum sexual encounters were seen as the level of success, to the whole consumer driven industry that first isolates you from everyone else because of lack of money and then the media industry that hooks you with sex and radicalism to hold your attention and these two together are very dangerous poisons for the mind.

I blame the schools for not teaching us in our teenage on how to control our attention and stay away from all these things, instead making "porn" a taboo topic rather than showing all it's negative impact on human mind and human life.

I blame them for not teaching me this:

1. Porn sends you into a loop of highs and lows and decreases your over all happiness levels as you get addicted to the highs more and more. So when you don't get porn most of

the time you feel very low. Just like a drug addict.

2. Porn creates unrealistic expectations from your love life, ruining your bond with your partner as you slowly stop enjoying actual sex as it doesn't feel wild enough like porn.
3. Porn makes you loose control over your impulses which flows down to other areas of your life, like loosing control over your impulse to eat more sugar, control over your impulse to become angry, control over your impulse to focus on studies without getting distracted. You become an impulse driven animal becoming fat, lazy, angry and unmotivated most of the time.
4. Porn makes you want to have multiple partners as you start seeing them as a tool to satisfy your sexual desire rather than a human being to connect with and build a bond and family with. You feel like the more tools you have to satisfy yourself the better. The modern generation even glorifies it by flaunting their "body counts". In the end this kind of lifestyle just makes you hollow from inside and you fall down to the level of an animal, driven by their wild needs rather

than a human who can build a beautiful life out of choice.

These are just some of many negative effects of porn on human mind I wish I was made aware of in my 20's. So yes I blame the society from big brands promoting consumerism, to media houses using sex as a tool to hook the audience, to our education systems not equipping us to fight this epidemic.

So being alone in my room, studying most of the time and watching some or the other kind of videos rest of the time got me hooked to porn. This is before the time I had a smartphone.

I just had my laptop which limited my access to porn just to my bedroom as whenever I was outside I didn't have a smartphone or the privacy to watch porn. So I became introspective and I noticed this loophole that I will stay away from porn as long as I stay outside my room.

Then I started studying in libraries day in and day out. I started volunteering with various societies to build robots and teach the juniors. This helped me with my grades and improved my social skills. This small introspection of how my body behaved in different environments saved my university life.

Now coming back to the modern time where I have the luxury of a small house, smart phone, income from a job and plenty of privacy, have I become mentally strong enough to resist porn completely? No. My fight with porn continues.

So now when I know a lot about human psychology and the effects of porn on my mind, do I still blame the society? No. Now whenever I fall into this loop I blame myself, I am responsible for making that informed choice.

So what am I doing to overcome this problem? First and foremost the hard work in school and university taught me to keep myself busy. Humans are the happiest when they are busy doing rather than busy thinking.

Does this mean I keep myself busy 24*7? Yes almost. But How? Don't I get tired of reading? Don't I get tired of working? Well we feel tired when we interpret something as work.

For example when someone tells you not to work and take rest, first impulse that comes to your mind is let's watch something. Because we have associated watching videos with relaxing.

What are videos in the end? Videos are just a bunch of people saying bunch of words and generating bunch of emotions in your mind, just the way I am doing with my words right now. So I interpreted reading books as watching videos through my imagination instead of work. This reframing helps me to pick up books instead of turning on any video device.

Similarly I added various activities in my day to keep my physically busy as well, like going for a 2 hours walk while listening to a podcast is my favourite go to activity which tires my body enough that I don't have the energy for porn when I come back, or going for swimming and maxing out my stamina in the swimming pool. These physical activities drain me and make me go to bed straight away.

Second and the most important thing is to stay away from all the sexual triggers during the day. Where do these sexual triggers come from? They come from the visual content that we watch. So how do I stay away from these triggers whenever I pick up my phone?

Firstly I sanitise my Instagram reels regularly to only show me the content that pushes me to work more, I do this by playing a certain kind of reel (Mahabharat reels) that I want to watch again and again. This sends a signal to the algorithm that this is the type of reel I want to watch and hence it shows me that.

Secondly not bringing my social media phone to my bed room. Invest in a basic whatsapp phone that you keep with yourself all the time, I am telling you it will be the best investment of your life.

The day you stop bringing your social media (Instagram/Youtube/Facebook) to your bedroom or any other place where it is not required, most of your problems will be solved. You will go to bed without scrolling and getting stimulated and you will wake up every morning without scrolling.

The more you stay away from mindless scrolling, the more you stay away from sexual triggers the media is trying to get you hooked into. The more you channelise your energy into achieving better

goals and forming better bonds with real human beings.

Now I have equipped you with the information and the solution, so if you still choose to loose your time to porn everyday, it will be your fault not society's.

Who Are You?

Essay 19

I have been recently asking this question to myself again and again. This is due to the anxiety of seeing others around me "living" a stable life whereas my own life seems to be a mess. I feel leaving my job to pursue my social media career and saying No to such a luxurious lifestyle which people crave for could put me decades behind, where getting to this financially comfortable position again might take me years.

All this fear is due to seeing my cousins and friends prospering and making me question my own identity. Who am I? What am I becoming? This pushed me into philosophy. And like always I found my answers there.

All this insecurity I have been feeling these days due to the fear of being left behind is due to over attachment to my identity. I am very attached to my identity "Daksh Jindal". But is that identity even real?

Who gave me this name? My parents. So the name was not my choice and then who fed the definition of success and failure into my mind? Society. So these definitions were not my choice.

So if tomorrow the whole world starts calling me "Rahul" and starts feeding me the new definition of success which is to become really good at dancing and the new definition of failure which is, someone who doesn't dance. Then even though I don't want to dance I will start dancing because society fed me these temporary definitions and gave me this temporary name.

So if my name can be changed, definition of success and failure can be changed. Then is there any point taking them seriously? Then what should I take seriously? Because the more I take my name seriously and these temporary definitions seriously, the more I want to defend my name by taking less risk to avoid bringing shame to my name because I feel my name is my identity.

The more I will want to chase the temporary definition of success set by the society because I will feel that is where happiness is because everyone says that.

Both attachment to the name and attachment to the temporary definitions of success brings mental disaster and anxiety in life. So this is where philosophy comes in, where it tells you to detach yourself from your name and from the temporary definitions of success and failure because they are not real.

Then what is real? Who am I? According to philosophy I am more than this body, mind and identity. I am pure energy, using this body and mind. I have no identity, which gives me the freedom to take any identity by surrendering.

Like when electric energy surrenders to a laptop it becomes a work machine, when it surrenders to a bulb it lights up the whole room. But that electric energy is neither the laptop nor the bulb. That electricity is pure energy. Similarly I am pure energy.

When I surrender to the work of engineering in front of me I become an engineer, when I surrender to writing this book I become a writer. But I am not an engineer nor a writer. So I should not take those identities seriously. The more I take them seriously the more I would want to defend them. Then in order to look like a good writer I will write only the things that people want to hear instead of the things I want to say. Similarly in order to look like a good engineer I will be scared of inventing anything new as I would fear that if I fail people won't see me as a good engineer. Attachment to our identity brings fear and anxiety.

So I won't take any identity seriously as none of those identities are real. Then what is real. The art of surrendering is real. Surrendering myself to engineering completely without fearing about success and failure and just enjoying building things no matter if it doesn't work. Just surrendering myself to write every honest word I can to help as many people I can is real. The art of surrendering is real.

Attachment to the identity is not real as that identity can be taken away from me anytime, tomorrow I meet with an accident and loose my fingers, I loose the identity of a writer. Or tomorrow I get laid off from the company I loose my identity of an engineer. Identity can be taken away from me anytime but no one can take away the art of surrendering from me.

Similarly these temporary definitions of success and failures can change at anytime, like 50 years back having a degree was success, 20 years back having a stable job was success now having a multi million dollar business is success. Tomorrow retiring with billion dollars might be success.

The definition of success will keep changing for the common man and they will keep running behind these new definitions like a lost traveller runs around the desert chasing mirage. These definitions are not real. Only the art of surrendering is real.

When you surrender you become water, you can take the shape of any vessel you are put into. You become someone who can surrender to any profession and become skilful because you don't love the temporary definitions of success and failure or the illusion of identity. You only love surrendering. Only the art of surrendering is real in the world of illusions.

So who are you? You are an energy who can completely surrender to anything that comes in it's way and take the shape of it. You are an energy who does not chase "names" and "identities". You are an energy who does not listen to the ever

changing definitions of success and failure spoken by the crowd. You are just an energy who completely surrenders to what comes in it's way.

Acknowledgements

I would like to thank Mohit Panchal (@itsbookgains) to help me decide the title and cover of the book. Thank you for proof reading and providing valuable feedbacks, your encouragement helped me to take this book more seriously.

I would also like to thank Renuka Gavarani (Best Selling author of The Art Of Being Alone) for proofreading the book and providing me valuable feedbacks.

I would also thank all my family and friends (mom, brother, sister, my girlfriend Sakshi) for all the support and freedom you gave me to write my first book.

In the end I would thank my biggest support group which are all my reader, followers, subscribers and podcast listeners who have made me realise that my words matter and they can change lives. Thank you so much for giving this stranger this opportunity and courage to change the world in a small way using his words.

Thank You

If you found this book helpful and you feel it can help the people around you, then don't feel shy to recommend them. Your recommendation can change the direction of their life.

Also it will help me in my mission to create a society with an action oriented mindset rather than an anxious society looking for the next new expensive thing and destroying their mental health, physical health, emotional health and the planet with their greed.

If you found the book relatable you can find more content from me on:

Spotify - The Mindset Show with Daksh Jindal
Youtube - Daksh Jindal
Instagram - @eardaksh

www.ingramcontent.com/pod-product-compliance
Lightning Source LLC
Chambersburg PA
CBHW031453150726
47990CB00007B/2744
* 9 7 9 8 8 9 5 1 9 4 1 6 4 *